The
Old
African

Ralph Wilkins

Atif Ananne Abdu Samsd

Table of contents

The Old African

Chapter 1- Page 3

Chapter 2- Page 21

Recounting The Old African

Chapter 3- Page 30

The Old African

Chapter 4- Page 39

By Ralph Wilkins

<u>Old African</u>

When times get hard and the world with its pressures mount up, I retreat into my personal fortress of solitude. A place where I am undisturbed, a place of cool

Contentment from the glaring sun and the eyes hiding in the night.

I reflect on the information I have absorbed over the years. The facts and the stories about my race and the tribulations heaped upon us over centuries. In

my place of repose. Where there is history, suffering, anguish, solitude and safety. This

place is old and of an unknown year.

A dilapidated, ramshackle of a shed.

It came with my old cottage styled

home. This old shed has weeds over growing on it's sides and rear. The front door is

off and lay buried on three corners by dirt and weeds. It's a small affair, about seven feet by twelve feet by eight feet and built from good old, sturdy wood.

It was constructed to last and it has.

When I first moved into my home, I went into the back yard and found this shed. It was drawing me to it. This treasure sat hidden, in plain sight. It's age and

style gave volumes of an age of craftsman that took pride in their work. It has

personality.

As old and worn out as it is, It has lasting

strength all about it. I fell in love

with it at first sight. I didn't know then that a close inspection of its inner space

would strike yet another cord within my being.

I would be bought to my knees in tears. I

would find myself once more at

the pathway to the past. A past overlooked by most of us.

I have for the past 37 years immersed myself in the study of my African roots. From my African homeland to my American captivity in this land which

exist on the woes of others. I consider myself a self-taught historian. Self-taught is the reading and studying every paper, essay and book written by my fellows. The

reality is, the idea of self-anything is a gross error. We are a people connected

forever by our history if nothing else.

Our history separates us from any other race. Our trials and tribulations

make our survival unique in human design. There has never been suffering like

ours. Suffering's foundation was laid

so well. Until today it's like all of the

yesterdays are going back, up to and beyond the "Willie Lynch" speech on the

James River so many years ago.

My small cottage styled house is in

Cedar Heights, in Prince George's County, Maryland. It is rumored to have been the quarters of the plantation's whip cracker. The term cracker is not racial, it's occupational. The history of this house goes back beyond the Civil War.

This whole area was a plantation or maybe even two. I don't know the

names of the plantations or of its owners. Not off hand anyway. I made a note to familiarize myself with this places history.

There were a lot of places like mine in this area. I seem to have the

distention of living on the sight of so much punishment and pain. This place of how many killings, rapes and de-humanizations? The place where slaves blood ran free

and their hopes were beaten down. Where their culture, language, religion and morals were taken from them. Where even the children were taken and ushered off to unknown destinations. I could feel the suffering like tiny pin pricks all over my body.

I could feel the past on me like a tight

blanket of pain. But even then I had no idea what was about to happen to me.

Something which would make firm in me the understanding and need to say more about what I knew.

In the corner of this shed like structure. I just kind of started to look around. I saw an old rusted piece of chain bolted to a stump or post. The post which at one time had been solidly buried in the ground was now rotted away at ground level had fallen into the far corner.

The chain was rusted into a stiff rope like line. One end was bolted to the post about 3 feet in length. The other was buried by the dust and debris of time.

The air in the shed was dry and dusty. The dim light left much to the imagination.

On the other end of chain was a large collar, revived and rusted closed. The iron collar was still heavy, solid and strong. There was this piece of wood inside of the collar when I lifted it out of the dust. As I lifted the collar from the debris and dust. Something fell from the ring, I caught it. I almost immediately knew that this object was not wood or stone. It was bone. It was eighteen inches or so and shaped on the ends like human bones. It looked like arm. The fore arm between the wrist and the elbow. It was human bone alright. My first thought was to call someone. Anyone because this looked like murder. Someone was chained up and left to die on this spot.

I realized in a flash just what I had found. This open grave, this shed was a place of supreme suffering of a slave.

It just came to me. I knew what it was, this shed of mine. I could see that this was old, very old. Maybe even over a hundred years old. These were the bones of a slave. I sat down on the cool earth and just followed the only rule I know to use at times like this. To stop and be still, to stop and just think.

My next move was to go into the house and get a flash light so I could further search the space. To see what other secrets could be found. With sweat on my brow

and tears in my eyes.
I found the rest of
this person.

Recounting the Old African

After the battle the old African had to flee,

to keep from becoming chattle and stolen to the sea.

Wounded with bleeding arm

With blood streaming down his face.

With the enemy giving chase sounding the alarm.

He and his warriors met the invaders. He and his fellows would have done better

If it were not for a traitor. He knew his

odds while
sharpening his knife,

He understood his mission, that he could lose his life.

He would never again would see his children or make love to his wife.

Yet here he was running out into the desert sun,

Out flanked and outnumbered forced by necessity to run.

After running hours in the desert heat,

He stumbles and falls, unable to stay on his feet.

The invader is no longer following his flight.

The oppressive heat is burning dehydrating and fooling his sight.

He knows that on this day the war must not die.

Many of the invaders
were killed.

Many of the invaders
women will lament
and cry.

Unable to fight then
to retreat into the
desert heat.

Knowing he will not
be a slave he prayed

that the buzzard that eats

him gets sick from his meat.

The old African never gave up and never quit.

They say the Creator saves the warrior.

To survive, regroup, find the invader once

more and continue to make

them pay.

Hunt him kill him by night and by day.

By Ralph Wilkins

38

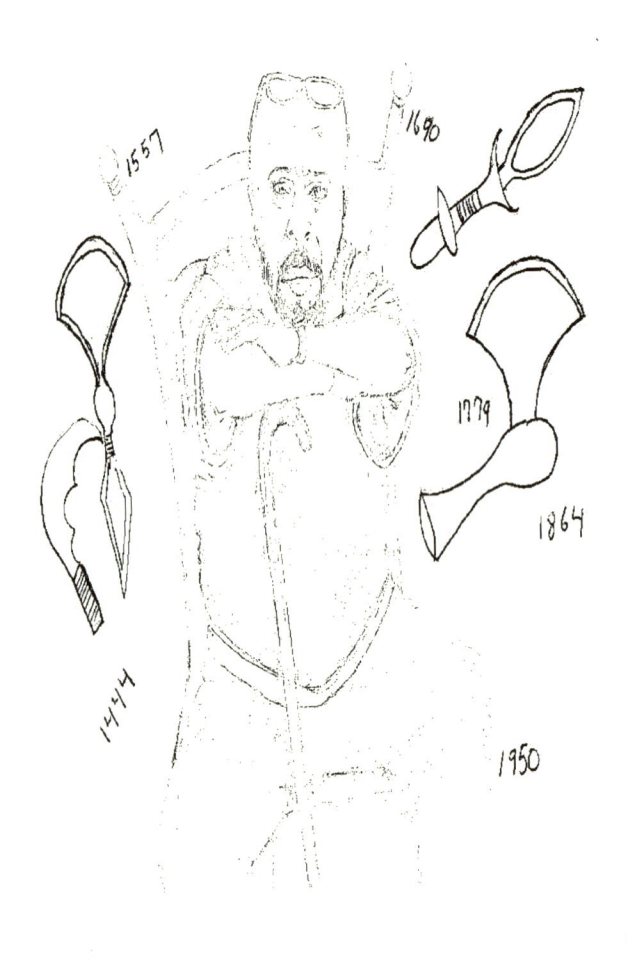

The Old African

Sadness knows that the Old African's revenge will go unanswered for yet another generation.

Overlooked and stepped on in his shallow grave. Be it water, dirt or dust from the sky. Who will avenge them? Who will dry the tears from the old African's eyes?

The black on black crime must fill his

heart with rage. Murdering each other over colors has no understanding. Disrespecting our leaders is the act of ignorant, insecure animals. When we find them in cages we question our own inactions.

Close your eyes and see five hundred African men, women and children chained together on a ship. See the captors give the order to lose the chains. See the cargo, slaves dragged by heavy weighted chains. They are chained at the ankle with iron. See them being dragged to the bottom of the ocean. Close your eyes and hear the screams taste the fear they must feel. Know the death they face. Know the death they face. Just because they are caught up in the claws of the

Germans, French, Spanish, Italians, Arabs and Other Africans, sold to Christians and Jews for a price. Sold For their labor as slaves. Sold to support the whole economy of nations. Just livestock not on the human scale.

You will never hear about the many that would flee, hide and fight rather than be a slave. This generation today will never know the pride of fighting back. They will never read about those which escaped and fought to the death. These misinformed, unguided and ignorant groups of youth will never embrace the truth. Why? Because they have become cowards and killers of self. Self in every form.

The old African asked questions about

everything. That made our civilization so great and our people such a prize. Mankind will never achieve the greatness of man.

By Ralph E. Wilkins

Atif Anane Abdus Samad

This writing is born of the insight and understanding gained over 67 years of living in the skin of a man blessed with the ability to truly see the realities of his existence.

Man is consumed by truth, reality and

distractions. If not for fear and ignorance hatred would have no life in the hearts of man.

Ralph Wilkins.

About the Author

Ralph Wilkins was born in 1950 in Washington, DC.

The forth boy of nine children. Raised in Fairmont Heights, Maryland.

His close family ties and his strict father gave

Him his foundation for life. A strict moral code, loyalty and

An above average IQ, with a never quit work ethic help

To make him who he is.

This writing The Old African, is one unit of Truth Teller, A collection

Writings written over 48 years. Short stories, poems and his auto biography.

Now on Amazon The Old African By Ralph Wilkins

Thank you for your support.

Ralph Wilkins

Atif Ananne Abdus Samad.

Made in the USA
Columbia, SC
12 June 2025